GOAL GETTERS

5 Steps to Finally Getting What You Want

NICOLE CRANK

STUDY GUIDE

Cover design by: Joe DeLeon
Cover photo by: Chosen Photography

ISBN: 978-1-950718-69-6   1 2 3 4 5 6 7 8 9 10

Printed in the United States of America

GOAL GETTERS

5 Steps to Finally Getting What You Want

NICOLE CRANK

STUDY GUIDE

AVAIL

CONTENTS

You're changing the way you think and it's going to change the way you live!

—NICOLE CRANK

Steak, Bones, and Hotdogs: Getting Your Dream Capacity Ready

"We've been settling for the leftovers. We've been surviving on just the scraps that come our way. Today, I want to encourage you. You're not living a "scraps" kind of life anymore." —Nicole Crank

Read Chapter 1 "Getting Ready" in *Goal Getters*, and reflect on the questions and discuss your answers with your study group.

In what areas of your life have you settled for the "bones" instead of the "steak" that God has for you? Explain your answer.

_____

_____

_____

_____

_____

_____

What do you think has been holding you back from identifying your goals?

_____

_____

_____

_____

_____

_____

REFLECT ON

Read Hebrews 116 (ESV)

"And without faith it is impossible to please him, for whoever would draw near to God must believe that he exists and that he rewards those who seek him."

What 'hot dog' goal or dream have you had that you're ready to upgrade to a 'steak' goal or dream?

_____

_____

_____

_____

_____

_____

_____

How does it make you feel to know that God can do more than you can ask or imagine—and that He wants to do it in your life?

_____

_____

_____

_____

_____

_____

_____

Looking at the "Five Simple Steps" that Nicole previews in this section, which one are you most excited to work on? Which one needs the most attention in your life right now?

_____

_____

_____

_____

_____

_____

_____

_____

How have you already seen God's plans for your life manifest themselves? How has He grown you, developed you, and used you already?

_____

_____

_____

_____

_____

_____

_____

_____

What practical steps are you going to take to get ready for this journey? It could be starting a planner, identifying a few key verses to write down and post somewhere, or finding an accountability partner.

_____

_____

_____

_____

_____

_____

_____

_____

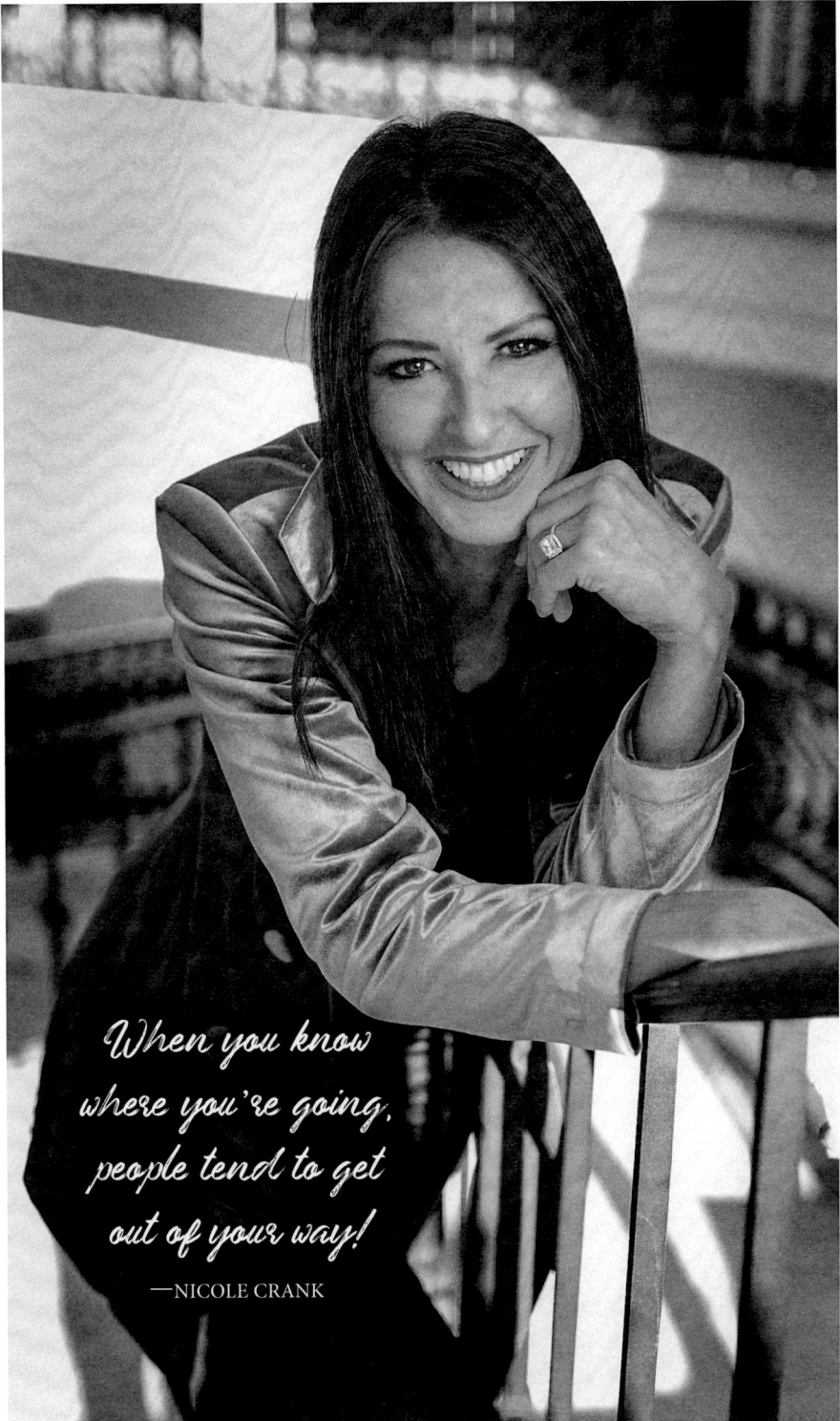

When you know
where you're going,
people tend to get
out of your way!

—NICOLE CRANK

Step One:

Set It and Get It: Dreaming and Setting Your Goals

"What would it take for this year to be the most amazing year of your life? That's the question we're going to answer with our goals."—Nicole Crank

Read "Step One Set It and Get It" in *Goal Getters*, and reflect on the questions and discuss your answers with your study group.

Have you ever caught yourself veering off-course when it comes to your goals and dreams? Why do you think this happened?

_____

_____

_____

_____

_____

_____

Why is it so essential to pray and get confirmation from God about the goals we set for ourselves? What do we risk when we skip this step?

_____

_____

_____

_____

_____

_____

REFLECT ON

Read Proverbs 36 (MSG)

*"Listen for God's voice in everything you do, everywhere you go;
He's the one who will keep you on track (or path)."*

In this section, we looked at Isaiah 55:8-9 (NIV). How does this truth about God's ways and thoughts affect our goal-setting process?

_____

_____

_____

_____

_____

_____

What are your goals? Take 3 minutes to pray and write them down—this will automatically increase the likelihood of reaching them!

1._____

_____

_____

2._____

_____

_____

3._____

_____

_____

4._____

_____

_____

5._____

_____

_____

6._____

_____

_____

7._____

_____

_____

8._____

_____

_____

9._____

_____

_____

Why do you think Pastor Nicole writes, "If the enormity of our dreams doesn't scare us just a little, then we may be walking by sight and not by faith"? Do your dreams intimidate you, or do you feel completely comfortable when you think about them?

_____

_____

_____

_____

_____

_____

_____

_____

_____

Look back at your list of goals. Are there any tweaks you can make so that they're more specific? What parameters, benchmarks, etc. can you add to make them measurable and attainable?

_____

_____

_____

_____

_____

_____

_____

_____

_____

Share your story on social media:

nicolecrank.com/letstalk

goalgetters

NicoleCrank

How are you feeling now that you have a concrete list of attainable goals written down?

_____

_____

_____

_____

_____

_____

Spend some more time praying and asking God to be with you and to bless these goals. Seek His confirmation as you move forward, and write any thoughts, words, or other notes below that you want to remember.

_____

_____

_____

_____

The shortest pencil is better than the longest memory. Write it down!
—NICOLE CRANK

Step Two:

Get a Vision: Turn Your Dreams into Goals

"Clarity is what we get when we turn our goals into a full-color, internalized vision."—Nicole Crank

Have you ever used visualization to gain clarity on your goals? If so, what did that look like? If not, how can you utilize this tool to help you move towards your goals?

_____

_____

_____

_____

_____

_____

_____

Why do you think so many people give up on their New Year's Resolutions so quickly?

_____

_____

_____

_____

_____

REFLECT ON

Read Isaiah 542-3 (ESV)

"Enlarge the place of your tent,
*   and let the curtains of your habitations be stretched out;*
do not hold back; lengthen your cords
*   and strengthen your stakes.*
For you will spread abroad to the right and to the left,
*   and your offspring will possess the nations*
*   and will people the desolate cities."*

Did anything about the neuroscience behind writing and re-writing your goals stand out to you in this chapter? How did the scientific aspect of this exercise shift your perspective?

_____

_____

_____

_____

_____

How is prioritizing time in the morning to write out your goals better than waiting until after you've accomplished other important tasks and to-dos?

_____

_____

_____

_____

_____

_____

Would you say that your past determines your future? Or do you operate relatively independently of your past? Explain your answer.

_____

_____

_____

_____

_____

_____

What will it take for you to not break down before you break-through in writing your goals on paper for 30 days? Visit nicolecrank.com/workbooks to access dozens of free, helpful worksheets!

_____

_____

_____

_____

_____

_____

Have you ever made a vision board? What excites you about this idea? Is there anything that intimidates you (remember, that's not a bad thing!)?

_____

_____

_____

_____

_____

_____

Based on this section, how does defining your goals empower you to believe God more—to grow your faith?

_____

_____

_____

_____

_____

Have you ever struggled to stay excited and motivated about your vision? Have you ever gotten bored? What tips from this chapter—or your own life—have you discovered to keep your passion alive?

_____

_____

_____

_____

_____

_____

_____

As you finish this chapter, what new insights, action steps, or other notes have you discovered that you want to remember?

_____

_____

_____

_____

_____

_____

_____

There is immense value is simply not quitting.
—NICOLE CRANK

Step Three:
Get Going: The Action Plan to Get You There

"You are the one who knows the tough questions in your own life. You know exactly where you want to grow and improve. So measure every metric and every item that has to do with your goal."—Nicole Crank

READING TIME

Read "Step Three Get Going" in *Goal Getters*, and reflect on the questions and discuss your answers with your study group.

Why is it so essential to define measurable goals? What risk do we run if our goals aren't measurable?

_____

_____

_____

_____

_____

_____

_____

Look back at the 7-10 goals you identified near the beginning of the study. Which aspects of them are measurable? What numbers, benchmarks, etc. have you identified for each one?

1._____

_____

_____

_____

_____

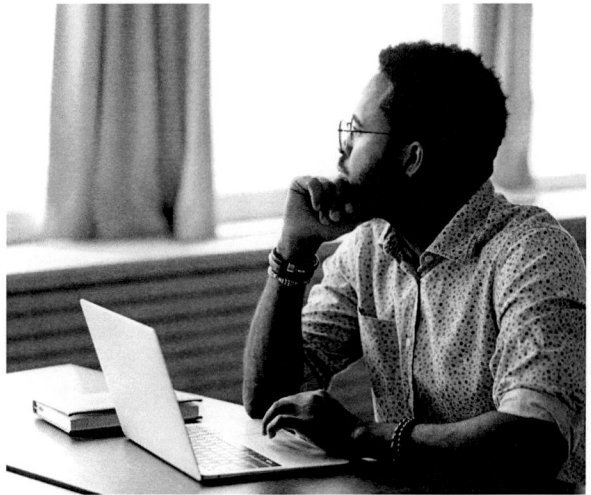

REFLECT ON

Read James 214 (MSG)

"Dear friends, do you think you'll get anywhere in this if you learn all the right words but never do anything?"

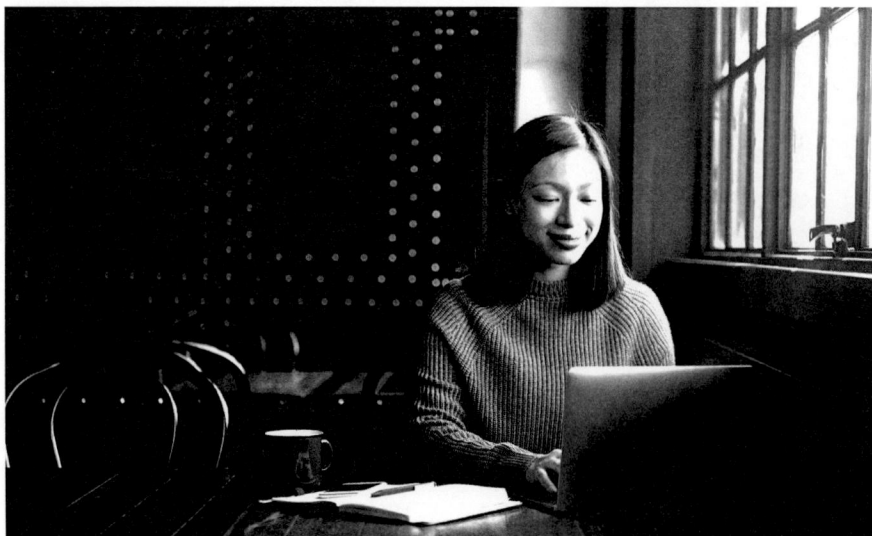

2._____

_____

_____

3._____

_____

_____

4._____

_____

_____

5._____

_____

_____

6._____

_____

_____

7._____

_____

_____

8._____

_____

_____

9._____

_____

_____

10._____

_____

_____

Explain the importance of assessing where you are right now. For each goal, make some notes about where you are and how you plan to move forward.

1._____

_____

_____

_____

2._____

_____

_____

_____

3._____

_____

_____

_____

4._____

_____

_____

_____

5._____

_____

_____

_____

6._____

_____

_____

7._____

_____

_____

8._____

_____

_____

9._____

_____

_____

10._____

_____

_____

Nicole lays out the importance of asking questions to get on your way to your goal. What additional questions can you come up with to ask yourself based on your specific goals?

_____

_____

_____

_____

_____

_____

How have you seen your goals and plans adjust in the past? How might you need to adjust them in the future?

_____

_____

_____

_____

_____

_____

_____

Do you find it easy to be flexible and adjust your goals, or is this difficult for you? Explain your answer.

_____

_____

_____

_____

_____

_____

_____

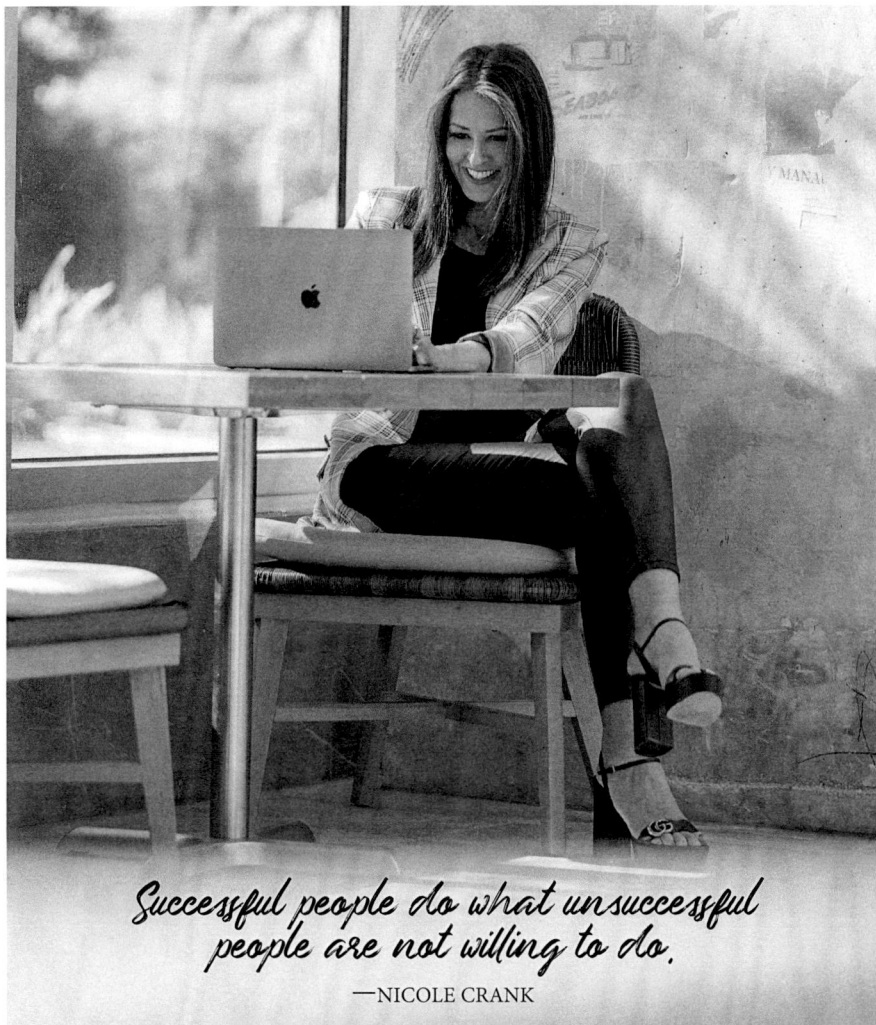

Successful people do what unsuccessful people are not willing to do.

—NICOLE CRANK

What are some of the "little pains" you'll need to commit to today in order to enjoy "big gains" tomorrow?

_____

_____

_____

_____

_____

_____

_____

Who can keep you accountable to the steps you've defined in this chapter? Think of 1-3 safe, supportive, and honest people who can speak into your life when you veer off course or compromise on the daily steps toward your goals—and who can cheer you on as you make progress!

1._____

_____

_____

2._____

_____

_____

3._____

_____

_____

Motivation gets you started; commitment delivers the package!

—NICOLE CRANK

What scares you most about reaching for these dreams? Why? Explain your answer.

_____

_____

_____

_____

_____

_____

_____

_____

_____

Step Four:

Get Results: The Benefits of Commitment

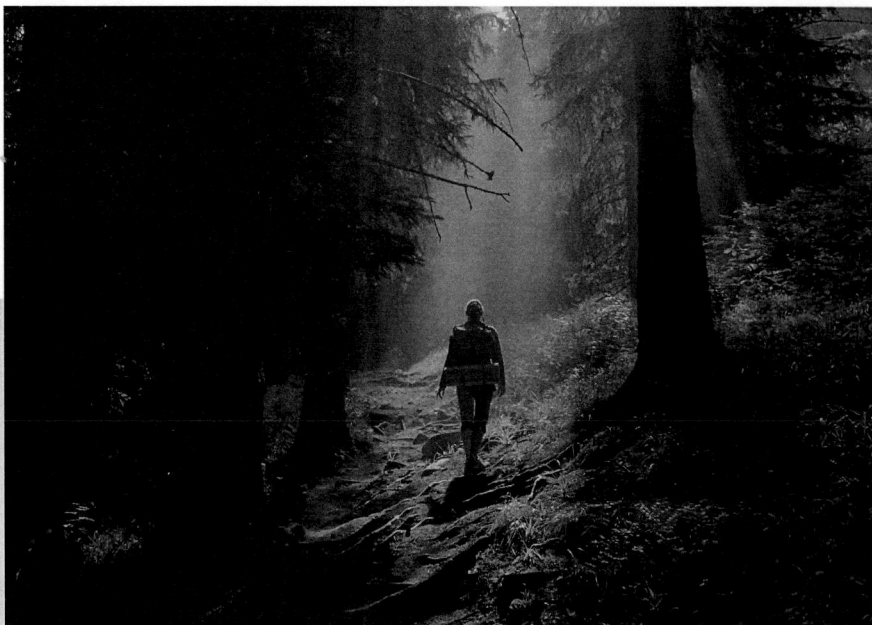

"Which way are you headed? Even if you've been distracted, or wandered completely off the path, you can turn around and start putting one foot in front of the other. That's all it takes to get back on track."—Nicole Crank

Read "Step Four Get Results" in *Goal Getters*, and reflect on the questions and discuss your answers with your study group.

Pick one of your goals and ask yourself, "Why are you doing what you're doing?" Write your answers and thoughts below.

_____

_____

_____

_____

_____

_____

_____

_____

How do you typically respond to setbacks, failures, or loss of momentum in pursuing your goals? Do you tend to get right back on track, or is it difficult for you to move on? Why do you think this is?

_____

_____

_____

_____

_____

_____

_____

_____

_____

_____

_____

_____

_____

REFLECT ON

Read 2 Peter 15 (AMP)

"For this very reason, adding your diligence [to the divine promises], employ every effort in exercising your faith to develop virtue (excellence, resolution, Christian energy), and in [exercising] virtue [develop] knowledge (intelligence)."

What are the biggest obstacles or struggles in your way right now?

_____

_____

_____

_____

_____

_____

What work might God be doing in the interim—the time between setting your goal and realizing it? Why is this season so important?

_____

_____

_____

_____

_____

_____

_____

How has failure actually moved you closer to your goals? How has it matured, grown, and developed you?

_____

_____

_____

_____

_____

_____

_____

Write down 5 reasons you WON'T give up!

1._____
_____
_____
_____
_____

2._____
_____
_____
_____
_____

3._____
_____
_____
_____
_____

4._____
_____
_____
_____
_____

5._____
_____
_____
_____

Write down 5 ways you'll get up one more time.

1._____

_____

_____

2._____

_____

_____

3._____

_____

_____

4._____

_____

_____

5._____

_____

_____

What we focus on tends to manifest.

—NICOLE CRANK

Write down 5 incentives you have to stay the course.

1._____

_____

_____

2._____

_____

_____

3._____

_____

_____

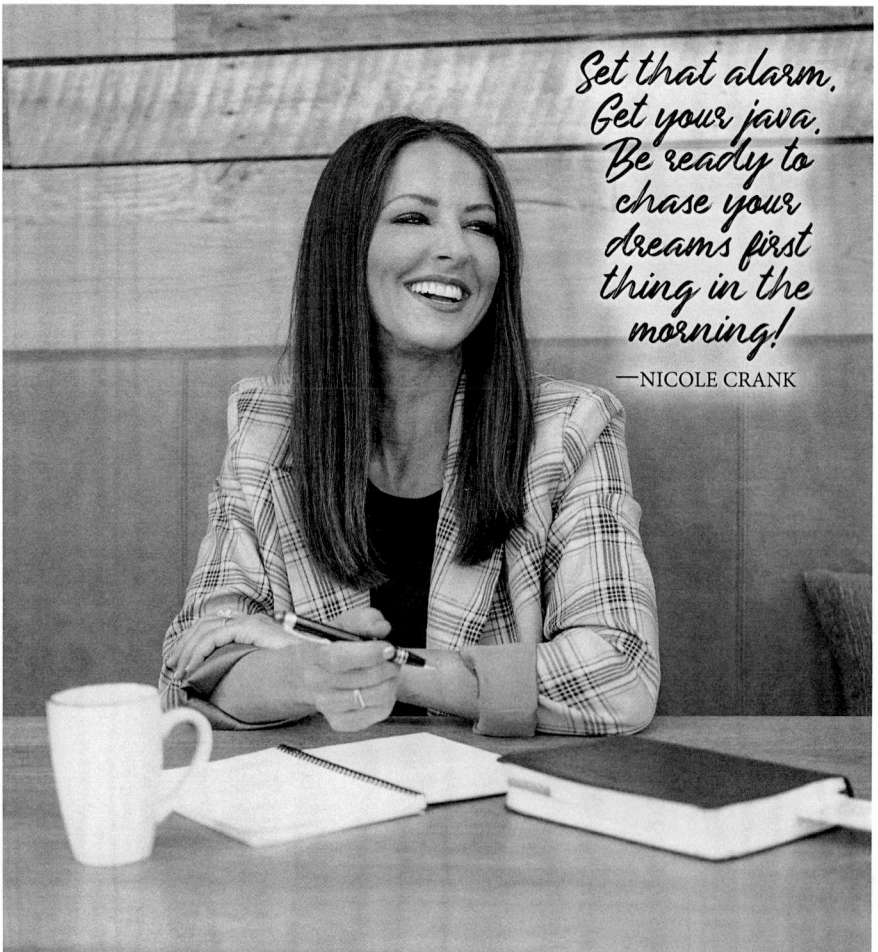

Set that alarm. Get your java. Be ready to chase your dreams first thing in the morning!

—NICOLE CRANK

4._____

_____

_____

5._____

_____

_____

What is God's part in fulfilling your goals? What is your part in reaching them?

_____

_____

_____

_____

_____

_____

_____

Who do you want to be part of your top five influencers?

1._____

_____

_____

2._____

_____

_____

3._____

_____

_____

4._____

_____

_____

5._____

_____

_____

_____

6._____

_____

_____

_____

7._____

_____

_____

_____

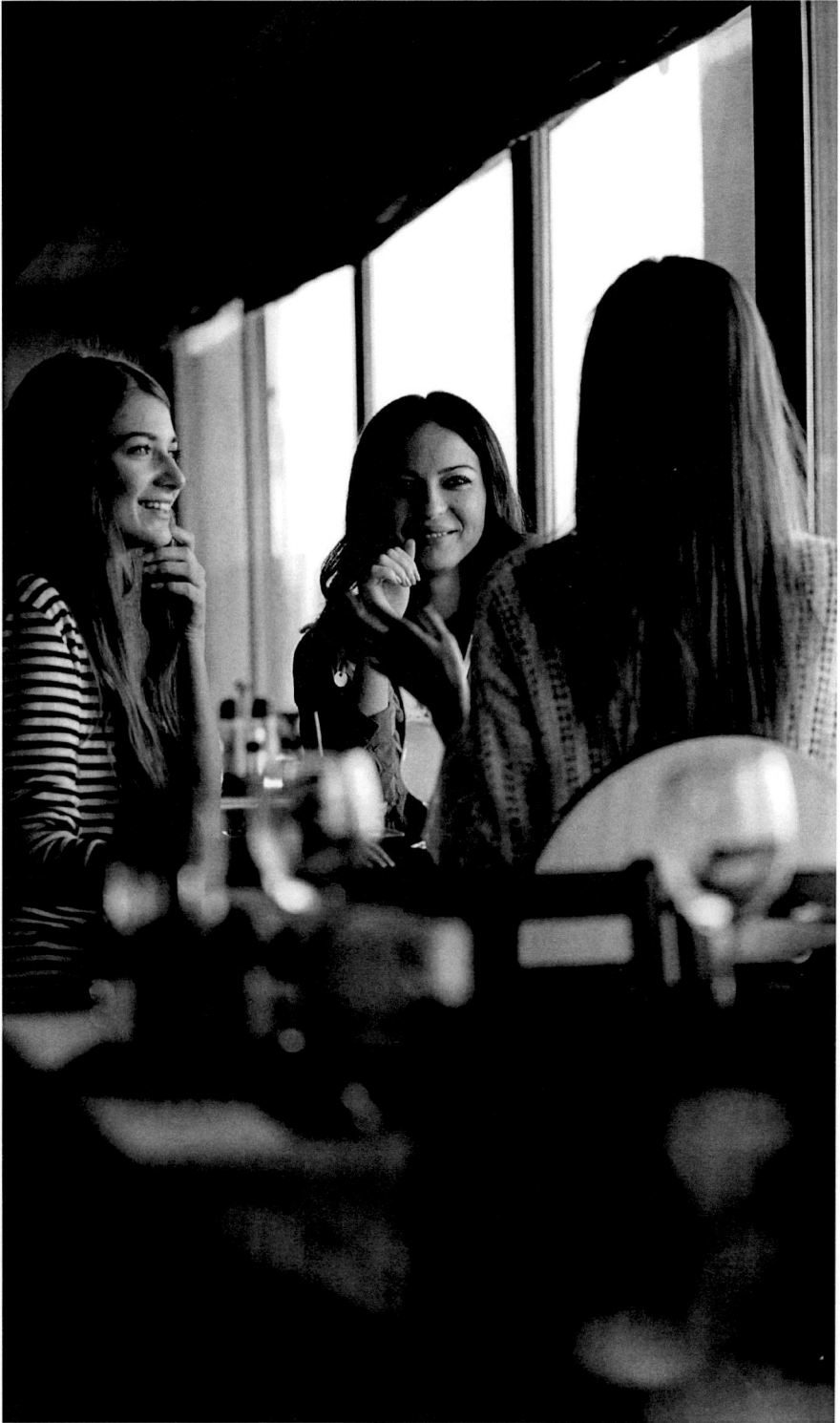

Step Five:

Get Happy: The Fuel of Taking Time to Enjoy the Reward

Consistency is the key to the breakthrough.

"You might not be where you want to be, but you're sure not where you used to be."—Nicole Crank

When it comes to rest, how are you doing in making time to rejuvenate, refresh, and reset? Where would you like to improve in this area?

_____

_____

_____

_____

_____

_____

Have you ever chosen a "good idea" over a "God idea"? How did you realize this? What did this experience teach you?

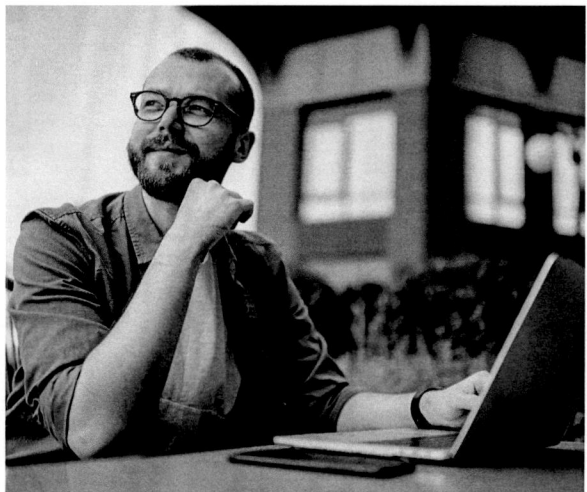

_____

_____

_____

_____

_____

Read Proverbs 215 (NIV)

"The plans of the diligent lead to profit as surely as haste leads to poverty."

What little, daily things do you do to pamper yourself? If you're not currently doing anything, what are some ideas that excite you?

_____

_____

_____

_____

_____

_____

_____

Do you struggle with guilt? In what ways? How can you combat any guilt that arises when you rest, celebrate, and reflect on your progress so far?

_____

_____

_____

_____

_____

_____

_____

What hobbies do you enjoy during your free time? What hobbies would you like to learn more about or spend more time doing?

_____

_____

_____

_____

_____

_____

Who helps you unwind, relax, and refresh yourself? Who are the healthy people in your life who encourage these rhythms?

_____

_____

_____

_____

_____

_____

_____

Do you know your love language? If so, what is it?

_____
_____
_____
_____
_____
_____
_____
_____
_____

What "little rewards" do you find most effective in encouraging you onward towards your long-term goal? For which benchmarks do you want to incorporate these rewards? Think of a couple of examples for each of your 7-10 goals.

1._____
_____
_____
_____
_____
_____

2._____
_____
_____
_____
_____

Our circumstances do not determine our destiny. Our decisions determine our destiny.

—NICOLE CRANK

Life isn't a sprint, it's a marathon. Run, REST ... run again!

—NICOLE CRANK

3._____

_____

_____

_____

4._____

_____

_____

_____

5._____

_____

_____

_____

6._____

_____

_____

_____

7._____

_____

_____

_____

8._____

_____

_____

9._____

_____

_____

10._____

_____

_____

_____

Bonus:

Get Tips, Tricks, and Hacks

"*Jesus was committed to His purpose. He stayed focused and maintained boundaries in order to keep His momentum towards His goal.*"—Nicole Crank

What hacks have you found that work best for you? Do you have a time of day or a certain place in which you're most motivated and productive? What routines, resources, and relationships have helped you grow and move towards your goals?

_____

_____

_____

_____

_____

_____

_____

Do you use to-do lists? What kind (paper, digital, app, etc.)?

_____

_____

_____

_____

_____

REFLECT ON

Read Ecclesiastes 910 (NLT)

"Whatever you do, do well. For when you go to the grave, there will be no work or planning or knowledge or wisdom."

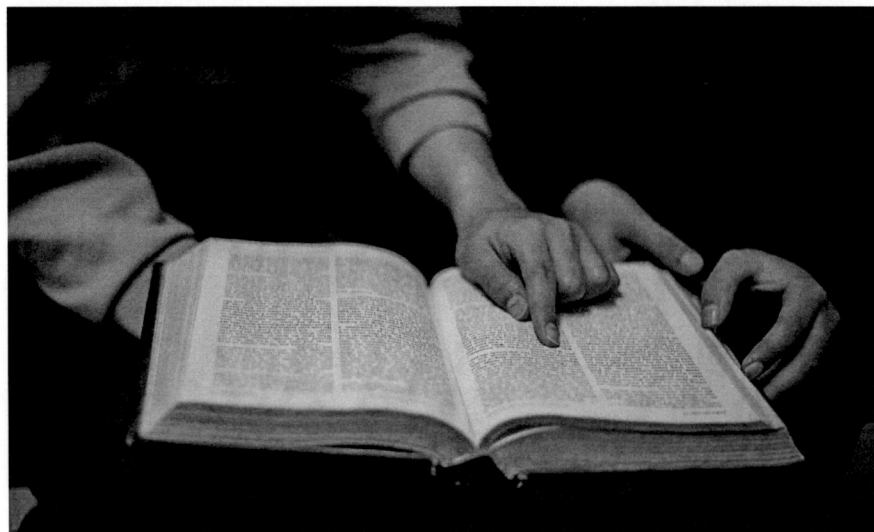

Which of the "6 Steps to Getting a Happy Routine" stuck out to you the most? How you can you work on this step in your life?

_____

_____

_____

_____

_____

_____

_____

_____

What areas of physical health do you need to improve upon?

_____

_____

_____

_____

_____

_____

_____

What about your mental and emotional health? What hacks or steps do you need to incorporate to stay well?

_____

_____

_____

_____

_____

_____

How have you seen "no" lead to a better "yes" in your life so far? What "nos" might you encounter as you pursue your goals?

_____

_____

_____

_____

_____

_____

What thing is God leading you to "subtract" from your life in order to move towards a more mature, healthier, and more successful place in Him?

_____

_____

_____

_____

_____

_____

Why is it a good thing that God doesn't choose us based on our worthiness? How does our willingness influence whether or not we fulfil the purposes He has for each one of us?

_____

_____

_____

_____

_____

_____

As you wrap up this study, what are action steps, thoughts, final insights, or other notes you want to remember?

_____

_____

_____

_____

_____

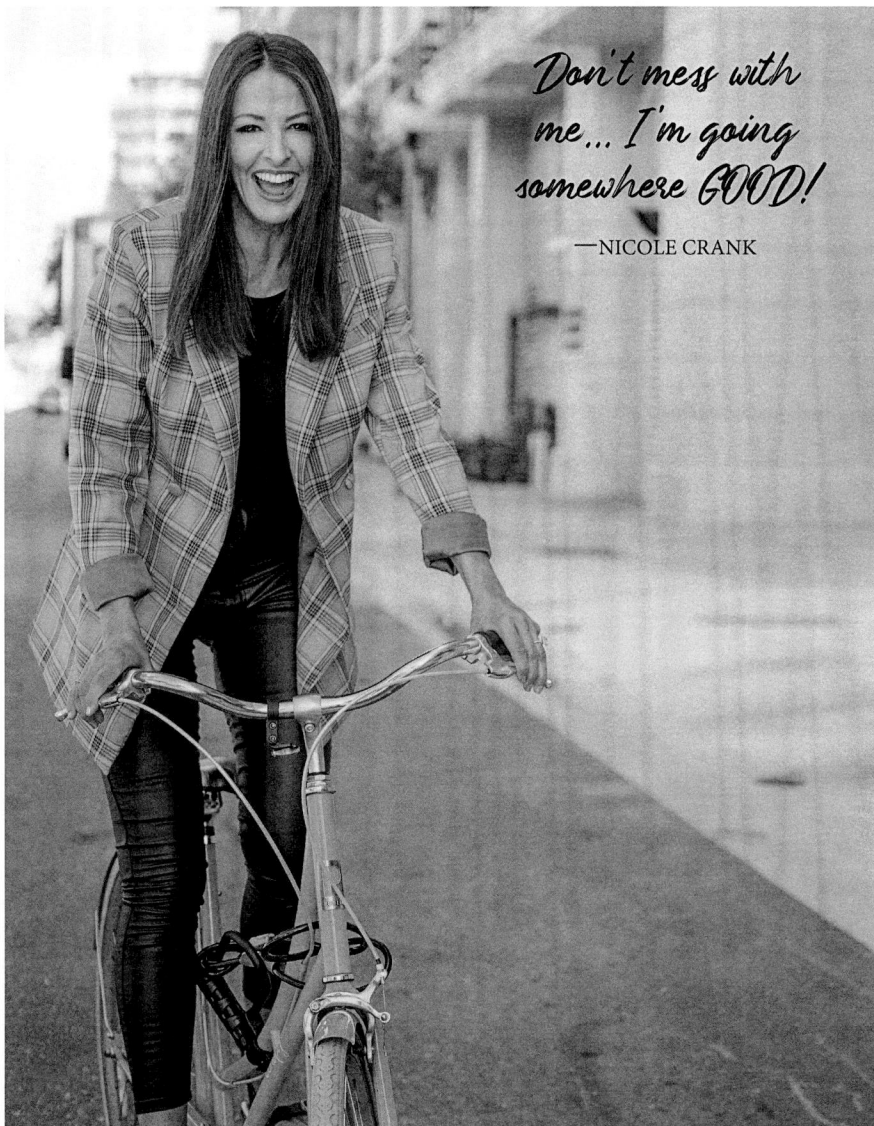

Don't mess with me... I'm going somewhere GOOD!

—NICOLE CRANK

Congratulations!

You've finished this Study Guide!

You're obviously a real Goal Getter!

Now—GET GOING!